CHRISTMAS

PENHALIGON'S
SCENTED TREASURY
OF VERSE AND
PROSE

CHRISTMAS

EDITED BY SHEILA PICKLES

HARMONY BOOKS
NEW YORK

FOR MY CHILDREN
JAMES AND CHARLOTTE ROSE

AND MY GODCHILDREN
SARAH, LOUISA, TAMSIN, RUPERT,
ALICE, GRACE AND SARAH

AND IN MEMORY OF ROSE.

⚞ INTRODUCTION ⚟

DEAR READER,
Christmas is a time for children and it brings out the child
in all of us. It has always been a very special time for me
and I still look forward to it and enjoy it tremendously. I
suspect this is because Christmas was made into a magical
occasion for Susan, my sister, and I as children, and my
enthusiasm and enjoyment now stem from creating this
magic for others.

When we were small, I remember the excitement
starting with writing to Father Christmas and gaining
momentum towards Christmas Day, just as D. H. Lawrence describes in *The Rainbow*. Then finally the great
day was spent surrounded by parcels and new toys, eating
huge meals with visiting relations, and much merriment
was had. As I grew up, Christmas Day itself became
something of an anticlimax. Perhaps this is because
children nowadays have high expectations of Christmas. I
know my children would be very disappointed to receive
only the one slim volume under their pillows which gave
such pleasure to Jo and her sisters in *Little Women*—this
is such a sharp contrast to the bonanza which Christmas
has become in many homes, and I cannot believe that it is
enjoyed any the more for it. On re-reading *A Christmas
Carol*, I was struck with guilt at modern expectations of

Christmas and resolved to re-read it each year at the beginning of December to keep Christmas in perspective and spare a thought for those less fortunate than ourselves, like the Cratchits. Interesting too that almost one hundred years ago George Bernard Shaw was rebelling against Christmas for its insincerity and vulgarity. Dickens writes that a man must be a misanthrope if he does not feel some joviality at the recurrence of Christmas and I would say that it is a poor-spirited creature indeed who feels no emotion at hearing the time-worn carols or finding a silver sixpence in his pudding.

It seems to me that with the emphasis there is today on partying and gift-giving, the reasons for celebrating Christmas are often lost and no one says this better than John Betjeman. I feel it is a wonderful opportunity to acknowledge friendships and show appreciation and, of course, spend time with family and friends. Part of the pleasure of Christmas for me is the tradition and familiarity of the rituals: the stirring of the pudding, the decorating of the tree, the filling of the stockings. Seeing the delight on the children's faces makes all the preparation worth while. After the stockings, the ideal Christmas Day continues with Matins, then hearth and home and relaxing with those dear to us. I have dedicated this book to those children who are dear to me in the hope that, as suggested by Elizabeth Bowen, Christmas happiness will always ring out in them like a peal of bells.

Sheila Pickles, Yorkshire 1989

⇥ HAPPY, HAPPY CHRISTMAS ⇤

CHRISTMAS time! That man must be a misanthrope indeed, in whose breast something like a jovial feeling is not roused – in whose mind some pleasant associations are not awakened – by the recurrence of Christmas. There are people who will tell you that Christmas is not to them what it used to be; that each succeeding Christmas has found some cherished hope, or happy prospect, of the year before, dimmed or passed away; that the present only serves to remind them of reduced circumstances and straitened incomes – of the feasts they once bestowed on hollow friends, and of the cold looks that meet them now, in adversity and misfortune. Never heed such dismal reminiscences. There are few men who have lived long enough in the world, who cannot call up such thoughts any day in the year. Then do not select the merriest of the three hundred and sixty-five for your doleful recollections, but draw your chair nearer the blazing fire – fill the glass and send round the song—and if your room be smaller than it was a dozen years ago, or if your glass be filled with reeking punch, instead of sparkling wine, put a good face on the matter, and empty it off-hand, and fill another, and troll off the old ditty you used to sing, and thank God it's no worse . . .

Who can be insensible to the outpourings of good feeling, and the honest interchange of affectionate attachment which abound at this season of the year. A Christmas family-party! We know nothing in nature more delightful! There seems a magic in the very name of Christmas. Petty jealousies and discords are forgotten; social feelings are awakened, in bosoms to which they have long been strangers; father and son, or brother and sister, who have met and passed with averted gaze, or a look of cold recognition, for months before, proffer and return the cordial embrace, and bury their past animosities in their present happiness. Kindly hearts that have yearned towards each other but have been withheld by false notions of pride and self-dignity, are again reunited, and all is kindness and benevolence! Would that Christmas lasted the whole year through (as it ought) and that the prejudices and passions which deform our better nature were never called into action among those to whom they should ever be strangers!

FROM *SKETCHES BY BOZ* BY CHARLES DICKENS, 1812–1870

◞❦ CHRISTMAS WAS COMING ❦◟

RADUALLY there gathered the feeling of expectation. Christmas was coming. In the shed, at nights, a secret candle was burning, a sound of veiled voices was heard. The boys were learning the old mystery play of St. George and Beelzebub. Twice a week, by lamplight, there was choir practice in the church, for the learning of old carols Brangwen wanted to hear. The girls went to these practices. Everywhere was a sense of mystery and rousedness. Everybody was preparing for something.

The time came near, the girls were decorating the church, with cold fingers binding holly and fir and yew about the pillars, till a new spirit was in the church, the stone broke out into dark, rich leaf, the arches put forth their æuds, and cold flowers rose to blossom in the dim, mystic atmosphere. Ursula must weave mistletoe over the door, and over the screen, and hang a silver dove from a sprig of yew, till dusk came down, and the church was like a grove.

In the cow-shed the boys were blacking their faces for a dress-rehearsal; the turkey hung dead, with opened, speckled wings, in the dairy. The time was come to make pies, in readiness.

The expectation grew more tense. The star was risen into the sky, the songs, the carols were ready to hail it. The star was the sign in the sky. Earth too should give a sign. As evening drew on, hearts beat fast with anticipation, hands were full of ready gifts. There were the tremulously expectant words of the church service, the night was past and the morning was come, the gifts were given and received, joy and peace made a flapping of wings in each heart, there was a great burst of carols, the Peace of the World had dawned, strife had passed away, every hand was linked in hand, every heart was singing.

FROM *THE RAINBOW* BY D. H. LAWRENCE, 1885–1930

—12—

⚬꙰ SNOWFALL ꙰⚬

IT was a fortnight before Christmas, and every one agreed that this would be a real Christmas, such as had not been seen for many years. There was a delightful cold nip in the air, as exhilarating as good news; the sky was grey and overcast, and the streets were covered with a thick layer of snow.

Few sights are more charming than that of a town covered with new-fallen, clean, white snow; and how pretty it is to watch the tiny flakes drift downward through the air as if there were a wedding in the sky and the fairies were throwing confetti.

At this time of the year the afternoons are short and the daylight quickly fades, so that the narrow streets which lead off the main roads of a great city like London assume an air more and more mysterious. The passer-by looks anxiously about him as his business takes him down some dark alley, for this is the season of goblins and pixies and elves—perhaps even the will-o'-the-wisps are in town.

FROM *THE MYSTERIOUS TOYSHOP* BY CYRIL W. BEAUMONT, 1891–1976

✤ CAROLS IN THE COTSWOLDS ✤

E approached our last house high up on the hill, the place of Joseph the farmer. For him we had chosen a special carol, which was about the other Joseph, so that we always felt that singing it added a spicy cheek to the night. The last stretch of country to reach his farm was perhaps the most difficult of all. In these rough bare lanes, open to all winds, sheep were buried and wagons lost. Huddled together, we tramped in one another's footsteps, powdered snow blew into our screwed-up eyes, the candles burned low, some blew out altogether, and we talked loudly above the gale.

Crossing, at last, the frozen millstream—whose wheel in summer still turned a barren mechanism—we climbed up to Joseph's farm. Sheltered by trees, warm on its bed of snow, it seemed always to be like this. As always it was late; as always this was our final call. The snow had a fine crust upon it, and the old trees sparkled like tinsel. We grouped ourselves round the farmhouse porch. The sky cleared, and broad streams of stars ran down over the valley and away to Wales. On Slad's white slopes, seen through the black sticks of its woods, some red lamps still burned in the windows.

Everything was quiet; everywhere there was the faint crackling silence of the winter night. We started singing, and we were all moved by the words and the sudden trueness of our voices. Pure, very clear, and breathless we sang:

> " As Joseph was a-walking
> He heard an angel sing,
> 'This night shall be the birth-time
> Of Christ the Heavenly King.

> " 'He neither shall be borned
> In Housen nor in hall,
> Nor in a place of paradise
> But in an ox's stall. . . .' "

And two thousand Christmases became real to us then; the houses, the halls, the places of paradise had all been visited; the stars were bright to guide the Kings through the snow; and across the farmyard we could hear the beasts in their stalls. We were given roast apples and hot mince pies, in our nostrils were spices like myrrh, and in our wooden box, as we headed back for the village, there were golden gifts for all.

FROM *CIDER WITH ROSIE*
BY LAURIE LEE, 1914–

GOOD CHRISTIAN MEN, REJOICE

Good Christian men, rejoice
  With heart and soul and voice!
  Now ye hear of endless bliss:
  Joy! Joy!
Jesus Christ was born for this.
He hath oped the heavenly door,
And man is blest for evermore.
  Christ was born for this.

JOHN MASON NEALE, 1818–1866

᪥ A Seasonable Sight ᪥

AT last the Rat succeeded in decoying him to the table, and had just got seriously to work with the sardine-opener when sounds were heard from the fore-court without— sounds like the scuffling of small feet in the gravel and a confused murmur of tiny voices, while broken sentences reached them—"Now, all in a line—hold the lantern up a bit, Tommy—clear your throats first—no coughing after I say one, two three.—Where's young Bill?—Here, come on, do, we're all a-waiting————"

"What's up?" inquired the Rat, pausing in his labours.

"I think it must be the field-mice," replied the Mole, with a touch of pride in his manner. "They go round carol-singing regularly at this time of the year. They're quite an institution in these parts. And they never pass me over—they come to Mole End last of all; and I used to give them hot drinks, and supper too sometimes, when I could afford it. It will be like old times to hear them again."

"Let's have a look at them!" cried the Rat, jumping up and running to the door.

It was a pretty sight, and a seasonable one, that met their eyes when they flung the door open. In the fore-court, lit by the dim rays of a horn lantern, some eight or ten little field-mice stood in a semi-circle, red worsted comforters round their throats, their fore-paws thrust deep into their pockets, their feet jigging for warmth. With bright beady eyes they glanced shyly at each other, sniggering a little, sniffing and applying coat-sleeves a good deal. As the door opened, one of the older ones that carried the lantern was just saying, "Now then, one, two, three!" and forthwith their shrill little voices uprose on the air, singing one of the old-time carols that their forefathers composed in fields that were fallow and held by frost, or when snow-bound in chimney corners, and handed down to be sung in the miry street to lamp-lit windows at Yule-time.

FROM *THE WIND IN THE WILLOWS* BY KENNETH GRAHAME, 1859-1932

The Holly and the Ivy

The Holly and the Ivy,
    When they are both full grown
Of all the trees are in the wood,
    The Holly bears the crown.

The Holly bears a blossom
    As white as any flower;
And Mary bore sweet Jesus Christ
    To be our sweet Saviour.

The Holly bears a berry
    As red as any blood;
And Mary bore sweet Jesus Christ
    To do poor sinners good.

The Holly bears a prickle
    As sharp as any thorn;
And Mary bore sweet Jesus Christ
    On Christmas in the morn.

The Holly bears a bark
    As bitter as any gall;
And Mary bore sweet Jesus Christ
    For to redeem us all.

The Holly and the Ivy
    Now both are full well grown:
Of all the trees are in the wood
    The Holly bears the crown.

Fifteenth-century English Carol

⟳ WINTER ⟳

A WRINKLED, crabbed man they picture thee,
  Old Winter, with a rugged beard as grey
As the long moss upon the apple-tree;
Blue lipt, an ice-drop at thy sharp blue nose;
  Close muffled up, and on thy dreary way,
Plodding alone through sleet and drifting snows.

They should have drawn thee by the high-heapt hearth,
  Old Winter! seated in thy great armed chair,
Watching the children at their Christmas mirth,
  Or circled by them, as thy lips declare
Some merry jest, or tale of murder dire,
  Or troubled spirit that disturbs the night,
Pausing at times to rouse the mouldering fire,
  Or taste the old October brown and bright.

ROBERT SOUTHEY, 1774–1843

❧ DECEMBER CHRISTMAS ❧

CHRISTMASS is come and every hearth
Makes room to give him welcome now
Een want will dry its tears in mirth
And crown him wi a holly bough
Tho tramping neath a winters sky
Oer snow track paths and ryhmey stiles
The huswife sets her spining bye
And bids him welcome wi her smiles

Neighbours resume their anual cheer
Wishing wi smiles and spirits high
Glad christmass and a happy year
To every morning passer bye
Milk maids their christmass journeys go
Accompanyd wi favourd swain
And childern pace the crumping snow
To taste their grannys cake again.

FROM *THE SHEPHERD'S CALENDAR*
BY JOHN CLARKE, 1609–1676

CHRISTMAS SHOPPING

HURCH Street was even busier, the good-humoured crowd so big that it spilled from the pavement on to the road. Shops were gay with Christmas decorations, fathers of families laden to the eyes with parcels made light of their burdens, genial old gentlemen carried turkeys and geese, and ladies merely smiled when, foolishly stopping to consult their last-minute lists, they were bumped into from all sides.

"Christians, awake, salute the happy morn," Kit grunted. "Well, good luck to 'em, I say. And," he added, groaning about the ordeal he still had to face, "an' to me an' all, judging by these grinning hordes."

Cursing himself for not having bought his presents sooner, he took a firm grip of his bag, and of the sack which held parts made at Mrs. Whittle's for the hand-gin, and joined the fray. An hour and a quarter later, by dint of much pushing and shoving, he had expended thirty-two shillings, twelve shilling of his own and the new sovereign which Atherton & Hesketh gave to their clerks as a Christmas Box. Well buffeted, he staggered out of Eastee's Toy Bazaar with a doll's tea-service for the Leigh twins tucked precariously under one arm, the remainder of his purchases clutched or stuffed elsewhere ... Mary Howitt's *Trust and Trial* which he had obtained for Belle in Howell's bookshop, a bottle of Gilbey's one-and-eight port from Hayes, a half-crown box of Lewis's special cigars, sundry other packages including a mounting set for Abel, and a false face and a pack of trick playing-cards for Luke, a pair of plated sugar-tongs, fiddle pattern, and, riding high out of his breast pocket, a copy of *Come into the Garden, Maud* which Judith would no doubt try out as soon as she got it.

FROM *KING COTTON* BY THOMAS ARMSTRONG, 1899–1978

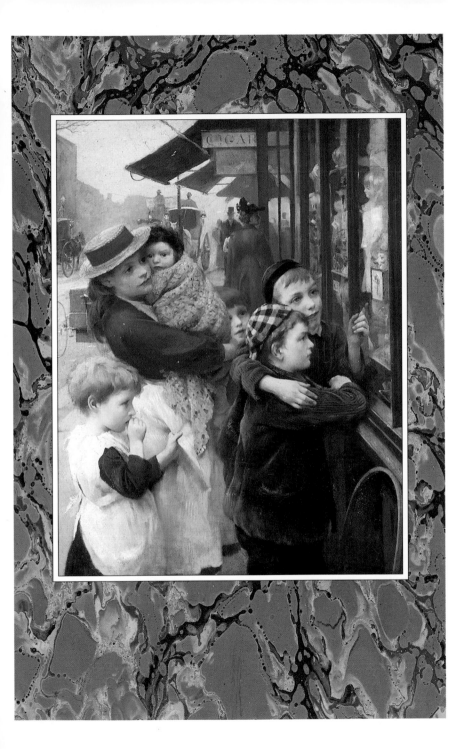

ᘒ. CHRISTMAS ᘒ

THE bells of waiting Advent ring,
The Tortoise stove is lit again
And lamp-oil light across the night
Has caught the streaks of winter rain
In many a stained-glass window sheen
From Crimson Lake to Hooker's Green.

The holly in the windy hedge
And round the Manor House the yew
Will soon be stripped to deck the ledge,
The altar, font and arch and pew,
So that the villagers can say
"The church looks nice" on Christmas Day.

Provincial public houses blaze
And Corporation tramcars clang,
On lighted tenements I gaze
Where paper decorations hang,
And bunting in the red Town Hall
Says "Merry Christmas to you all"

And London shops on Christmas Eve
  Are strung with silver bells and flowers
As hurrying clerks the City leave
  To pigeon-haunted classic towers,
And marbled clouds go scudding by
The many-steepled London sky.

And girls in slacks remember Dad,
  And oafish louts remember Mum,
And sleepless children's hearts are glad,
  And Christmas-morning bells say "Come!"
Even to shining ones who dwell
Safe in the Dorchester Hotel.

And is it true? And is it true,
  This most tremendous tale of all,
Seen in a stained-glass window's hue,
  A Baby in an ox's stall?
The Maker of the stars and sea
Become a Child on earth for me?

And is it true? For if it is,
  No loving fingers tying strings
Around those tissued fripperies,
  The sweet and silly Christmas things,
Bath salts and inexpensive scent
And hideous tie so kindly meant,

No love that in a family dwells,
  No carolling in frosty air,
Nor all the steeple-shaking bells
  Can with this single Truth compare-
That God was Man in Palestine
And lives to-day in Bread and Wine.

JOHN BETJEMAN, 1906–1984

CHRISTMAS IN OLDEN TIME

THE fire, with well-dried logs supplied,
　Went roaring up the chimney wide;
The huge hall-table's oaken face,
Scrubb'd till it shone, the day to grace,
Bore then upon its massive board
No mark to part the squire and lord.
Then was brought in the lusty brawn,
By old blue-coated serving-man;
Then the grim boar's head frown'd on high,
Crested with bays and rosemary.
Well can the green-garb'd ranger tell,
How, when, and where, the monster fell;
What dogs before his death he tore,
And all the baiting of the boar.
The wassel round, in good brown bowls,
Garnish'd with ribbons, blithely trowls.
There the huge sirloin reek'd; hard by
Plum-porridge stood, and Christmas pie;
Nor fail'd old Scotland to produce,
At such high tide, her savoury goose.
Then come the merry maskers in,
And carols roar'd with blithesome din;
If unmelodious was the song,
It was hearty note, and strong.
Who lists may in their mumming see
Traces of ancient mystery;
White shirts supplied the masquerade,
And smutted cheeks the visors made;
But, O! what maskers, richly dight,
Can boast of bosoms half so light!
England was merry England, when
Old Christmas brought his sports again.
'Twas Christmas broach'd the mightiest ale;
'Twas Christmas told the merriest tale;
A Christmas gambol oft could cheer
The poor man's heart through half the year.

SIR WALTER SCOTT. 1771–1832

✎ A Hansom Cab ✎

NATURALLY Tony wanted to see the shops, and as soon as the Christmas holidays began I was allowed to go with her and mother to the West End. Tony was all for taking hansoms. As she pointed out, a bus can be taken any day—a holiday was a holiday, and she didn't believe in doing things by halves. She argued that it is the regular expenses that one should worry about, not the occasional. So she took hansoms right and left, and I can still recall the luxurious feeling of snuggling down in a hansom between her and mother, to be wafted exactly where we wanted to go. I could just see the toss of the horse's head and could hear the klip-klop of his hoofs and the cheerful jingle of his bells. It is amusing to reflect now that the bells on a hansom were put there as a warning to pedestrians to get out of the way of such swift vehicles. Those were the days when a man with a red flag used to walk in front of a steam-roller. I wonder what Tony would say to the traffic in Piccadilly to-day. On one of her later visits to London I took her on the top of a bus, to see some of the life of the town. As I called her attention to this and that, she said, "Don't ask me to look, dear. If I take my eye off the driver he will surely run into something."

FROM *A LONDON CHILD OF THE 1870S* BY M. V. HUGHES. 1866–1956

A BOHEMIAN CHRISTMAS

Schaunard
And now what are you doing?
No! These victuals
are in store
for the dark
days ahead.
(putting everything in the cupboard:)
Dine at home on Christmas Eve
while the streets of the Latin Quarter
are festooned with sausages and tit-bits?
When the smell of fritters
pervades those old streets?
There, young girls are singing happily . . .

Rodolfo, Marcello, Colline
Christmas Eve!

Schaunard
. . . and each has a student
for echo!
Let's observe tradition, gentlemen:
we'll drink at home, but let's eat out!

FROM THE LIBRETTO OF *LA BOHÈME*
BY GIACOMO PUCCINI, 1858–1924

A COUNTRY PARSON'S
CHRISTMAS EVE

RITING Christmas letters all the morning. In the afternoon I went to the church with Dora and Teddy to put up Christmas decorations. Dora had been very busy for some days past making the straw letters for the Christmas text. Fair Rosamund and good Elizabeth Knight came to the church to help us and worked heartily and well. They had made some pretty ivy knots and bunches for the pulpit panels and the ivy blossoms cleverly whitened with flour looked just like white flowers.

The churchwarden Jacob Knight was sitting by his sister in front of the roaring fire. We were talking of the death of Major Torrens on the ice at Corsham pond yesterday. Speaking of people slipping and falling on ice the good churchwarden sagely remarked, "Some do fall on their faces and some do fall on their rumps. And they as do hold their selves uncommon stiff do most in generally fall on their rumps."

I took old John Bryant a Christmas packet of tea and sugar and raisins from my Mother. The old man had covered himself almost entirely over in his bed to keep himself warm, like a marmot in its nest. He said, "If I live till New Year's Day I shall have seen ninety-six New Years." He said also, "I do often see things flying about me, thousands and thousands of them about half the size of a large pea, and they are red, white, blue, and yellow and all colours. I asked Mr Morgan what they were and he said they were the spirits of just men made perfect."

FROM *DIARY 1870–1879* BY THE REV. FRANCIS KILVERT

THE OXEN

CHRISTMAS Eve, and twelve of the clock.
  "Now they are all on their knees,"
  An elder said as we sat in a flock
By the embers in hearthside ease.

We pictured the meek mild creatures where
They dwelt in their strawy pen,
Nor did it occur to one of us there
To doubt they were kneeling then.

So fair a fancy few would weave
In these years! Yet, I feel,
If someone said on Christmas Eve,
"Come; see the oxen kneel

"In the lonely barton by yonder coomb
Our childhood used to know,"
I should go with him in the gloom,
Hoping it might be so.

THOMAS HARDY, 1840–1928

MEDITATION ON CHRISTMAS EVE

NIGHT has fallen; the clear, bright stars are sparkling in the cold air; noisy, strident voices rise to my ear from the city, voices of the revelers of this world who celebrate with merrymaking the poverty of their Saviour. Around me in their rooms my companions are asleep, and I am still wakeful, thinking of the mystery of Bethlehem.

Come, come, Jesus, I await you.

Mary and Joseph, knowing the hour is near, are turned away by the townsfolk and go out into the fields to look for a shelter. I am a poor shepherd; I have only a wretched stable, a small manger, some wisps of straw. I offer all these to you, be pleased to come into my poor hovel. I offer you my heart; my soul is poor and bare of virtues, the straws of so many imperfections will prick you and make you weep—but oh, my Lord, what can you expect? This little is all I have. I am touched by your poverty, I am moved to tears, but I have nothing better to offer you, Jesus, honour my soul with your presence, adorn it with your graces. Burn this straw and change it into a soft couch for your most holy body.

Jesus, I am here waiting for your coming. Wicked men have driven you out, and the wind is like ice. I am a poor man, but I will warm you as well as I can. At least be pleased that I wish to welcome you warmly, to love you and sacrifice myself for you.

These moving words were written on Christmas Eve, 1902, by a young Italian named Angelo Giuseppe Roncalli who was studying for the priesthood in Rome. Two years later he graduated as a doctor in theology and was ordained. The world now remembers him as the widely beloved Pope John XXIII.

─❊ THE CHRISTMAS EVE SUPPER ❊─

"**T**HE Christmas Eve supper! Oh no, I shall never go
in for that again!" Stout Henri Templier said that
in a furious voice, as if someone had proposed some crime
to him, while the others laughed and said:

"What are you flying into a rage about?"

"Because a Christmas Eve supper played me the
dirtiest trick in the world, and ever since I have felt an
insurmountable horror for that night of imbecile gaiety."

"Tell us about it."

"You want to know what it was? Very well then, just
listen.

"You remember how cold it was two years ago at
Christmas; cold enough to kill poor people in the streets.

The Seine was covered with ice; the pavements froze one's feet through the soles of one's boots, and the whole world seemed to be at the point of congealing.

"I had a big piece of work on and refused every invitation to supper, as I preferred to spend the night at my writing table. I dined alone and then began to work. But about ten o'clock I grew restless at the thought of the gay and busy life all over Paris, at the noise in the streets which reached me in spite of everything, at my neighbors' preparation for supper which I heard through the walls. I hardly knew any longer what I was doing; I wrote nonsense, and at last I came to the conclusion that I had better give up all hope of producing any good work that night.

"I walked up and down my room; I sat down and got up again. I was certainly under the mysterious influence of the enjoyment outside, and I resigned myself to it. So I rang for my servant and said to her:

"'Angela, go and get a good supper for two: some oysters, a cold partridge, some crayfish, ham and some cakes. Put out two bottles of champagne, lay the cloth and go to bed.'

"She obeyed in some surprise, and when all was ready I put on my greatcoat and went out. The great question remained: 'Whom was I going to bring in to supper?' My female friends had all been invited elsewhere, and if I had wished to have one I ought to have seen about it beforehand. So I thought that I would do a good action at the same time and said to myself:

"'Paris is full of poor and pretty girls who will have nothing on the table tonight and who are on the lookout for some generous fellow. I will act the part of providence to one of them this evening, and I will find one if I have to go to every pleasure resort, and I will hunt till I find one to my choice.' So I started off on my search...."

GUY DE MAUPASSANT, 1850–1893

❧ A VISIT FROM ST NICHOLAS ❧

DOWN the chimney St. Nicholas came with a bound.
He was dressed all in fur from his head to his foot,
And his clothes were all tarnished with ashes and soot;
A bundle of toys he had flung on his back,
And he looked like a peddler just opening his pack.
His eyes how they twinkled! his dimples how merry!
His cheeks were like roses, his nose like a cherry;
His droll little mouth was drawn up like a bow,
And the beard on his chin was as white as the snow.
The stump of a pipe he held tight in his teeth,
And the smoke it encircled his head like a wreath.
He had a broad face, and a little round belly
That shook, when he laughed, like a bowl full of jelly.
He was chubby and plump,—a right jolly old elf—
And I laughed when I saw him, in spite of myself.
A wink of his eye and a twist of his head
Soon gave me to know I had nothing to dread.
He spoke not a word, but went straight to his work,
And filled all the stockings; then turned with a jerk,
And laying his finger aside of his nose,
And giving a nod, up the chimney he rose.
He sprang to his sleigh, to his team gave a whistle,
And away they all flew like the down of a thistle;
But I heard him exclaim, ere he drove out of sight:
"Happy Christmas to all, and to all a good-night!"

CLEMENT CLARKE MOORE, 1779–1863

❦. AND IT CAME TO PASS ❧

AND Joseph also went up from Galilee, out of the city of Nazareth, into Judæa, unto the city of David, which is called Bethlehem; (because he was of the house and lineage of David:)

To be taxed with Mary his espoused wife, being great with child.

And so it was, that, while they were there, the days were accomplished that she should be delivered.

And she brought forth her first-born son, and wrapped him in swaddling clothes, and laid him in a manger; because there was no room for them in the inn.

And there were in the same country shepherds abiding in the field, keeping watch over their flock by night.

And, lo, the angel of the Lord came upon them, and the glory of the Lord shone round about them: and they were sore afraid.

And the angel said unto them, Fear not: for, behold, I bring you good tidings of great joy, which shall be to all people.

For unto you is born this day in the city of David a Saviour, which is Christ the Lord.

THE GOSPEL ACCORDING TO ST. LUKE, 2

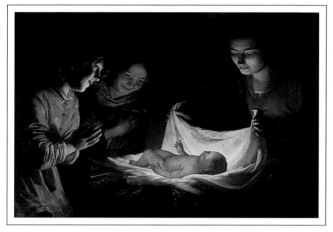

⊶❦ A CHRISTMAS CAROL ❦⊷

THE Christ-child lay on Mary's lap,
His hair was like a light,
(O weary, weary were the world,
But here is all aright.)

The Christ-child lay on Mary's breast,
His hair was like a star.
(O stern and cunning are the kings,
But here the true hearts are.)

The Christ-child lay on Mary's heart,
His hair was like a fire.
(O weary, weary is the world,
But here the world's desire.)

The Christ-child stood at Mary's knee,
His hair was like a crown,
And all the flowers looked up at him,
And all the stars looked down.

G. K. CHESTERTON, 1874–1936

Small Boy. And then the Presents?

Self. And then the Presents, after the Christmas box. And the cold postman, with a rose on his button-nose, tingled down the teatray-slithered run of the chilly glinting hill. He went in his ice-bound boots like a man on fishmonger's slabs. He wagged his bag like a frozen camel's hump, dizzily turned the corner on one foot, and, by God, he was gone.

Small Boy. Get back to the Presents.

Self. There were the Useful Presents: engulfing mufflers of the old coach days, and mittens made for giant sloths; zebra scarves of a substance like silky gum that could be tug-o'-warred down to the goloshes; blinding tam-O'-shanters like patchwork tea-cosies, and bunnyscutted busbies and balaclavas for victims of headshrinking tribes; from aunts who always wore wool-next-to-the-skin, there were moustached and rasping vests that made you wonder why the aunties had any skin left at all; and once I had a little crocheted nose-bag from an aunt now, alas, no longer whinnying with us. And pictureless books in which small boys, though warned, with quotations, not to, *would* skate on Farmer Garge's pond, and did, and drowned; and books that told me everything about the wasp, except why.

Small Boy. Get on to the Useless Presents.

Self. On Christmas Eve I hung at the foot of my bed Bessie Bunter's black stocking, and always, I said, I would stay awake all the moonlit, snowlit night to hear the roof-alighting reindeer and see the hollied boot descend through soot. But soon the sand of the snow drifted into my eyes, and, though I stared towards the fireplace and around the flickering room where the black sack-like stocking hung, I was asleep before the chimney trembled and the room was red and white with Christmas. But in

the morning, though no snow melted on the bedroom floor, the stocking bulged and brimmed; press it, it squeaked like a mouse-in-a-box; it smelt of tangerine; a furry arm lolled over, like the arm of a kangaroo out of its mother's belly; squeeze it hard in the middle, and something squelched; squeeze it again—squelch again. Look out of the frost-scribbled window: on the great loneliness of the small hill, a blackbird was silent in the snow.

Small Boy. Were there any sweets?

Self. Of course there were sweets. It was the marshmallows that squelched. Hardboileds, toffee, fudge and allsorts, crunches, cracknels, humbugs, glaciers, and marzipan and butterwelsh for the Welsh. And troops of bright tin soldiers who, if they would not fight, could always run. And Snakes-and-Families and Happy Ladders. And Easy Hobbi-Games for Little Engineers, complete with Instructions. Oh, easy for Leonardo! And a whistle to make the dogs bark to wake up the old man next door to make him beat on the wall with his stick to shake our picture off the wall. And a packet of cigarettes: you put one in your mouth and you stood at the corner of the street and you waited for hours, in vain, for an old lady to scold you for

smoking a cigarette and then, with a smirk, you ate it. And, last of all, in the toe of the stocking, sixpence like a silver corn. And then downstairs for breakfast under the balloons!

FROM *A PROSPECT OF THE SEA*
BY DYLAN THOMAS, 1914–1953

⸙ CHRISTMAS MORNING ⸙

Jo was the first to wake in the gray dawn of Christmas morning. No stockings hung at the fireplace, and for a moment she felt as much disappointed as she did long ago, when her little sock fell down because it was so crammed with goodies. Then she remembered her mother's promise, and slipping her hand under her pillow, drew out a little crimson-covered book. She knew it very well, for it was that beautiful old story of the best life ever lived, and Jo felt that it was a true guide-book for any pilgrim going the long journey. She woke Meg with a "Merry Christmas," and bade her see what was under her pillow. A green-covered book appeared, with the same picture inside, and a few words written by their mother, which made their one present very precious in their eyes. Presently Beth and Amy woke, to rummage and find their little books also,—one dove-colored, the other blue; and all sat looking at and talking about them, while the east grew rosy with the coming day.

FROM *LITTLE WOMEN* BY LOUISA MAY ALCOTT, 1832–1888

❧ A LETTER FROM SANTA CLAUS ❧

Palace of St. Nicholas
In the Moon
Christmas Morning

MY DEAR SUSIE CLEMENS:

I have received and read all the letters which you and your little sister have written me by the hand of your mother and your nurses; I have also read those which you little people have written me with your own hands—for although you did not use any characters that are in grown peoples' alphabet, you used the characters that all children in all lands on earth and in the twinkling stars use; and as all my subjects in the moon are children and use no character but that, you will easily understand that I can read your and your baby sister's jagged and fantastic marks without any trouble at all. But I had trouble with those letters which you dictated through your mother and the nurses, for I am a foreigner and cannot read English writing well. You will find that I made no mistakes about the things which you and the baby ordered in your own letters—I went down your chimney at midnight when you were asleep and delivered them all myself—and kissed both of you, too, because you are good children, well trained, nice mannered, and about the most obedient little people I ever saw.

MARK TWAIN, 1835-1910

❧ CHRISTMAS VICTUALS ❧

Now thrice welcome, Christmas,
   Which brings us good cheer,
Minced pies and plum porridge,
   Good ale and strong beer;
With pig, goose and capon,
   The best that may be,
So well doth the weather
   And our stomachs agree.

Observe how the chimneys
   Do smoke all about,
The cooks are providing
   For dinner, no doubt;
But those on whose tables
   No victuals appear,
O may they keep Lent
   All the rest of the year.

SEVENTEENTH-CENTURY ENGLISH CAROL

℘ CHRISTMAS PUDDING ℘

INGREDIENTS. – ½ lb. of beef suet, 2 ozs. of flour, ½ lb. of raisins, ¼ lb. of mixed peel, ½ a grated nutmeg, ½ oz. of mixed spice, ½ oz. of ground cinnamon, 1 gill of milk, 1 wineglassful of rum or brandy, ½ lb. of breadcrumbs, ½ lb. of sultanas, ¼ lb. of currants, 1 lemon, 2 ozs. of desiccated cocoanut or shredded almonds, a pinch of salt, 4 eggs.

METHOD. – Skin the suet and chop it finely. Clean the fruit, stone the raisins, finely shred the mixed peel; peel and chop the lemon-rind. Put all the dry ingredients in a basin and mix well. Add the milk, stir in the eggs one at a time, add the rum or brandy, and the strained juice of the lemon. Work the whole thoroughly for some minutes, so that the ingredients are well blended. Put the mixture in a well-buttered basin or pudding-cloth; if the latter is used it should be buttered or floured. Boil for about 4 hours, or steam for at least 5 hours.

AVERAGE COST. – 1s. 10d. SUFFICIENT for 8 or 9 persons.

MRS BEETON, 1836–1865

⤙❊❈ TURKEY, ROASTED ❈❊⤚

INGREDIENTS.—1 turkey, 1 to 2 lbs. of sausage meat, 1 to 1½ lbs. of veal forcemeat, 2 or 3 slices of bacon, 1 pint of good gravy, bread sauce, fat for basting.

METHOD.—Prepare and truss the turkey. Fill the crop with sausage meat, and put the veal forcemeat inside the body of the bird. Skewer the bacon over the breast, baste well with hot fat, and roast in front of a clear fire or in a moderate oven from 1¾ to 2¼ hours, according to age and size of the bird. Baste frequently, and about 20 minutes before serving remove the bacon to allow the breast to brown. Remove the trussing strings, serve on a hot dish, and send the gravy and bread sauce to table in sauce boats.

TIME.—From 1¾ to 2¼ hours. AVERAGE COST, 10s. to 16s. SEASONABLE from September to February.

MRS BEETON, 1836–1865

THE GOOSE

UCH a bustle ensued that you might have thought a
goose the rarest of all birds; a feathered phenomenon,
to which a black swan was a matter of course—and in
truth it was something very like it in that house. Mrs.
Cratchit made the gravy (ready beforehand in a little
saucepan), hissing hot; Master Peter mashed the potatoes
with incredible vigour; Miss Belinda sweetened up the
apple-sauce; Martha dusted the hot plates; Bob took Tiny
Tim beside him in a tiny corner at the table; the two
young Cratchits set chairs for everybody, not forgetting
themselves, and mounting guard upon their posts,
crammed spoons into their mouths, lest they should shriek
for goose before their turn came to be helped. At last the
dishes were set on, and grace was said. It was succeeded by
a breathless pause, as Mrs. Cratchit, looking slowly all
along the carving-knive, prepared to plunge it in the
breast; but when she did, and when the long expected gush
of stuffing issued forth, one murmur of delight arose all
round the board, and even Tiny Tim, excited by the two
young Cratchits, beat on the table with the handle of his
knife, and feebly cried Hurrah!

FROM *A CHRISTMAS CAROL* BY CHARLES DICKENS, 1812–1870

CHRISTMAS DAY 1661

25TH (CHRISTMAS DAY.) Had a pleasant walk to White Hall, where I intended to have received the Communion with the family, but I come a little too late. So I walked up into the house, and spent my time looking over pictures, particularly the ships in King Henry the VIIIth's voyage to Bullaen; marking the great difference between those built then and now. By and by down to the chapel again, where Bishop Morley preached upon the song of the Angels, 'Glory to God on high, on earth peace and good will towards men.' Methought he made but a poor sermon, but long, and, reprehending the common jollity of the Court for the true joy that shall and ought to be on these days, he particularized concerning their excess in playes and gaming, saying that he whose office it is to keep the gamesters in order and within bounds, serves but for a second rather in a duell, meaning the groome-porter. Upon which it was worth observing how far they are come from taking the reprehensions of a bishop seriously, that they all laugh in the chapel when he reflected on their ill actions and courses. He did much press us to joy in these public days of joy, and to hospitality; but one that stood by whispered in my eare that the Bishop do not spend one groate to the poor himself. The sermon done, a good anthem followed with vialls, and the King come down to receive the Sacrament. But I staid not, but calling my boy from my Lord's lodgings, and giving Sarah some good advice by my Lord's order to be sober, and look after the house, I walked home again with great pleasure, and there dined by my wife's bed-side with great content, having a mess of brave plum-porridge and a roasted pullet for dinner, and I sent for a mince-pie abroad, my wife not being well, to make any herself yet.

SAMUEL PEPYS, 1633–1703

GLOUCESTERSHIRE WASSAIL

WASSAIL, Wassail, all over the town!
Our toast it is white, and our ale it is brown,
Our bowl it is made of the white maple tree;
With the wassailing bowl we'll drink to thee.

And here is to Dobbin and to his right eye,
Pray God send our master a good Christmas pie,
And a good Christmas pie that may we all see;
With our wassailing bowl we'll drink to thee . . .

TRADITIONAL

❧ GOD BLESS US EVERY ONE ☙

ALLO! A great deal of steam! The pudding was out of the copper. A smell like a washing-day! That was the cloth. A smell like an eating-house and a pastrycook's next door to each other, with a laundress's next door to that! That was the pudding! In half a minute Mrs Cratchit entered—flushed, but smiling proudly—with the pudding, like a speckled cannon-ball, so hard and firm, blazing in half of half-a-quartern of ignited brandy, and bedight with Christmas holly stuck into the top.

Oh, a wonderful pudding! Bob Cratchit said, and calmly too, that he regarded it as the greatest success achieved by Mrs Cratchit since their marriage. Mrs Cratchit said that now the weight was off her mind, she would confess she had had her doubts about the quantity of flour. Everybody had something to say about it, but nobody said or thought it was at all a small pudding for a large family. It would have been flat heresy to do so. Any Cratchit would have blushed to hint at such a thing.

At last the dinner was all done, the cloth was cleared, the hearth swept, and the fire made up. The compound in the jug being tasted, and considered perfect, apples and oranges were put upon the table, and a shovel-full of chestnuts on the fire. Then all the Cratchit family drew round the hearth, in what Bob Cratchit called a circle, meaning half a one; and at Bob Cratchit's elbow stood the family display of glass. Two tumblers, and a custard-cup without a handle.

These held the hot stuff from the jug, however, as well as golden goblets would have done; and Bob served it out with beaming looks, while the chestnuts on the fire sputtered and cracked noisily. Then Bob proposed:

" A Merry Christmas to us all, my dears. God bless us!"

Which all the family re-echoed.

"God bless us every one!" said Tiny Tim, the last of all.

FROM *A CHRISTMAS CAROL* BY CHARLES DICKENS, 1812–1870

⤙✖ A CHRISTMAS TREE ✖⤙

I HAVE been looking on, this evening, at a merry company of children assembled round that pretty German toy, a Christmas Tree. The tree was planted in the middle of a great round table, and towered high above their heads. It was brilliantly lighted by a multitude of little tapers; and everywhere sparkled and glittered with bright objects. There were rosy-cheeked dolls, hiding behind the green leaves; and there were real watches (with movable hands, at least, and an endless capacity of being wound up) dangling from innumerable twigs; there were French-polished tables, chairs, bedsteads, wardrobes, eight-day clocks, and various other articles of domestic furniture (wonderfully made, in tin, at Wolverhampton), perched among the boughs, as if in preparation for some fairy housekeeping; there were jolly, broad-faced little men, much more agreeable in appearance than many real men—and no wonder, for their heads took off, and showed them to be full of sugar-plums; there were fiddles and drums; there were tambourines, books, work-boxes, paint-boxes, sweetmeat boxes, peep-show boxes, and all kinds of boxes; there were trinkets for the elder girls, far brighter than any grown-up gold and jewels; there were baskets and pincushions in all devices; there were guns, swords, and banners; there were witches standing in enchanted rings of pasteboard, to tell fortunes; there were teetotums, humming-tops, needle-cases, pen-wipers, smelling-bottles, conversation-cards, bouquet-holders; real fruit, made artificially dazzling with gold leaf; imitation apples, pears, and walnuts, crammed with surprises; in short, as a pretty child, before me, delightedly whispered to another pretty child, her bosom friend, "There was everything, and more."

FROM *CHRISTMAS STORIES* BY CHARLES DICKENS, 1812–1870

৵৶ OUR CHRISTMAS AT HOME ৲৴

E had been very merry all day, and, as soon as the lights were brought in at tea-time, we came trooping into the parlour from all parts of the house—some from the dairy, where Mary had been making butter; others from the nursery, where they had been playing at soldiers; and the rest from the apple-store over the stable and the school-room, then used only as a play-room, it being holiday time.

We were all assembled in the parlour, and, after tea, my mother told us that we might have a game at romps. We needed no second bidding, and so to play we went in good earnest. We played at Hunt the Slipper and Forfeits, and I don't know how many other games, till we were called into the kitchen for a dance. A good old country dance it was, in which the family, servants, and all joined, noisily enough—all but my mother, who sat under a sort of arbour of holly and other green leaves—for there were always plenty of green leaves and red berries to be got in the garden and orchard, however severe the winter might be—and encouraged us with kind words and beaming smiles. After we were tired of dancing—which was not soon, I assure you—a great china bowl of raisins was brought in by John the butler, who acted occasionally as gardener and coachman as well, and was, in fact, a sort of Jack-of-all-trades. What fun there was, to be sure as we ran dancing and singing round the lighted bowl, snatching the plums from the blue flames of the burning spirit, till they were all gone and the blue flames burned

themselves out. Well, Snap-dragon over, we had kisses under the Mistletoe; and I recollect quite well how we all laughed when Papa took Betty the cook under the white-berried bough and gave her a great loud kiss.

But our fun had not yet ended. At a signal from my mother we followed her into the dining-room on the other side of the passage. Here a sight awaited us that surprised us one and all. The room was brilliantly lighted up with wax candles on sconces from the walls; and on the table in the centre there was placed a great Christmas Tree, hung all over with little lamps and bon-bons, and toys and sweetmeats and bags of cakes. It was the first tree of the kind that I and my companions had ever seen. It was quite a new-fashion the Christmas Tree; and my brother Tom, who had just come home from Germany, had super-intended its getting up and decoration. With what shouts of joy we hailed the pretty Christmas Tree, and with what glee and laughter we began to search among its twinkling lights and bright green leaves for the toys and sweetmeats that were hanging there, each one with a name written on its envelope, I can hardly tell you. But we were very merry, I know, and very grateful to our dear mother for her care in providing this delightful surprise as a finish to our merry evening's sports.

ANONYMOUS, *THE CHRISTMAS TREE*, 1857

❧ BLIND MAN'S BUFF ☙

E shall have sport when Christmas comes,
When "snap-dragon" burns our fingers and thumbs:
We'll hang mistletoe over our dear little cousins,
And pull them beneath it and kiss them by dozens:
We shall have games at "Blind Man's Buff,"
And noise and laughter and romping enough.

We'll crown the plum-pudding with bunches of bay,
And roast all the chestnuts that come in our way;
And when Twelfth Night falls, we'll have such a cake
That as we stand round it the table shall quake.
We'll draw "King and Queen," and be happy together,
And dance old "Sir Roger" with hearts like a feather.
Home for the Holidays, here we go!
But this Fast train is really exceedingly slow!

HOME FOR THE HOLIDAYS, ANONYMOUS

CHRISTMAS DAY AT SEA

I N all my twenty years of wandering over the restless waters of the globe I can only remember one Christmas Day celebrated by a present given and received. It was, in my view, a proper live-sea transaction, no offering of Dead Sea fruit; and in its unexpectedness perhaps worth recording....

The daybreak of Christmas Day in the year 1879 was fine. The sun began to shine sometime about four o'clock over the somber expanse of the Southern Ocean in latitude 51; and shortly afterwards a sail was sighted ahead. The wind was light, but a heavy swell was running. Presently I wished a "Merry Christmas" to my captain. He looked sleepy, but amiable. I reported the distant sail to him and ventured the opinion that there was something wrong with her. He said, "Wrong?" in an incredulous tone. I pointed out that she had all her upper sails furled and that she was brought to the wind, which, in that region of the world, could not be accounted for on any other theory....

The captain, as is a captain's way, disappeared from the deck; and after a time our carpenter came up the poop ladder carrying an empty small wooden keg, of the sort in which certain ship's provisions are packed. I said, surprised, "What do you mean by lugging this thing up here, Chips?"

"Captain's orders, sir," he explained shortly.

I did not like to question him further, and so we only exchanged Christmas greetings and he went away. The next person to speak to me was the steward. He came running up the companion stairs. "Have you any old newspapers in your room, sir?"

We had left Sydney, N.S.W., eighteen days before. There were several old Sydney *Heralds*, *Telegraphs*, *Bulletins* in my cabin, besides a few home papers received by the last mail. "Why do you ask, steward?" I inquired naturally.

"The captain would like to have them," he said.

And even then I did not understand the inwardness of these eccentricities. I was only lost in astonishment at them. It was eight o'clock before we had closed with that ship, which, under her short canvas and heading nowhere in particular, seemed to be loafing aimlessly on the very threshold of the gloomy home of storms. But long before that hour I learned from the number of boats she carried that this nonchalant ship was a whaler. She had hoisted the Stars and Stripes at her peak, and her signal flags had already told us that her name was *Alaska*—two years out from New York—east from Honolulu—two hundred and fifteen days on the cruising ground.

We passed, sailing slowly, within a hundred yards of her; and just as our steward started ringing the breakfast bell, the captain and I held aloft, in good view of the figures watching us over her stern, the keg, properly headed up and containing, besides an enormous bundle of newspapers, two boxes of figs in honor of the day. We flung it far out over the rail. Instantly our ship, sliding down the slope of a high swell, left it far behind in our wake. On board the *Alaska* a man in a fur cap flourished an arm; another, a much bewhiskered person, ran forward suddenly. I never saw anything so ready and so smart as the way that whaler, rolling desperately all the time, lowered one of her boats. The Southern Ocean went on tossing the two ships like a juggler his gilt balls, and the microscopic white speck of the boat seemed to come into the game instantly, as if shot out from a catapult on the enormous and lonely stage. That Yankee whaler lost not a moment in picking up her Christmas present from the English wool clipper.

FROM *CHRISTMAS DAY AT SEA* BY
JOSEPH CONRAD, 1857–1924

☙ AN ATROCIOUS INSTITUTION ❧

The World, 20 December 1893

LIKE all intelligent people, I greatly dislike Christmas. It revolts me to see a whole nation refrain from music for weeks together in order that every man may rifle his neighbour's pockets under cover of a ghastly general pretence of festivity. It is really an atrocious institution, this Christmas. We must be gluttonous because it is Christmas. We must be drunken because it is Christmas. We must be insincerely generous; we must buy things that nobody wants, and give them to people we don't like; we must go to absurd entertainments that make even our little children satirical; we must writhe under venal officiousness from legions of freebooters, all because it is Christmas—that is, because the mass of the population, including the all-powerful middle-class tradesman, depends on a week of licence and brigandage, waste and intemperance, to clear off its outstanding liabilities at the end of the year.

GEORGE BERNARD SHAW, 1856–1950

✥. OF STOUT AND STUFFING ✥

ABRIEL took his seat boldly at the head of the table and, having looked to the edge of the carver, plunged his fork firmly into the goose. He felt quite at ease now for he was an expert carver and liked nothing better than to find himself at the head of a well-laden table.

"Miss Furlong, what shall I send you?" he asked. "A wing or a slice of the breast?"

"Just a small slice of the breast."

"Miss Higgins, what for you?"

"O, anything at all, Mr Conroy."

While Gabriel and Miss Daly exchanged plates of goose and plates of ham and spiced beef Lily went from guest to guest with a dish of hot floury potatoes wrapped in a white napkin. This was Mary Jane's idea and she had also suggested apple sauce for the goose but Aunt Kate had said that plain roast goose without apple sauce had always been good enough for her and she hoped she might never eat worse. Mary Jane waited on her pupils and saw that they got the best slices and Aunt Kate and Aunt Julia opened and carried across from the piano bottles of stout and ale for the gentlemen and bottles of minerals for the ladies. There was a great deal of confusion and laughter and noise, the noise of orders and counter-orders, of knives and forks, of corks and glass-stoppers. Gabriel began to carve second helpings as soon as he had finished the first round without serving himself. Every one protested loudly so that he compromised by taking a long draught of stout for he had found the carving hot work. Mary Jane settled down quietly to her supper but Aunt Kate and Aunt Julia were still toddling round the table, walking on each other's heels, getting in each other's way and giving each other unheeded orders. Mr Browne begged of them to sit down and eat their suppers and so did Gabriel but they said there was time enough so that, at

last Freddy Malins stood up and, capturing Aunt Kate,
plumped her down on her chair amid general laughter.

When everyone had been well served Gabriel said,
smiling:

"Now, if anyone wants a little more of what vulgar
people call stuffing let him or her speak."

A chorus of voices invited him to begin his own supper
and Lily came forward with three potatoes which she had
reserved for him.

"Very well," said Gabriel amiably, as he took another
preparatory draught, "kindly forget my existence, ladies
and gentlemen, for a few minutes."

FROM "THE DEAD" BY JAMES JOYCE, 1882–1941

❧ THE KISSING BUNCH ❧

"GREY rabbit! He's been! Wake up! He's been in the night!"

"Who?" cried Grey Rabbit, rubbing her eyes and sitting up in a fright. "Who? Has Rat been?"

"Santa Claus!" cried Hare, capering up and down by her bed. "Be quick and come downstairs and see the surprises."

Grey Rabbit dressed hurriedly, but there was a little twinkle in her eyes as she entered the room.

"Look what he brought me!" cried Squirrel, holding out a pair of fur mittens and bedroom slippers made from sheep's wool.

"And he gave me a spotted handkerchief, and a musical box," cried Hare excitedly, and he turned the handle of the little round box from which came a jolly tune which set their feet dancing.

"Look at the Kissing Bunch!" Hare went on. "Isn't it lovely! Let's all kiss under it."

So they gave their Christmas morning kisses under the round Christmas Bunch in the time-honoured way.

FROM *LITTLE GREY RABBIT'S CHRISTMAS* BY ALISON UTTLEY, 1884–1976

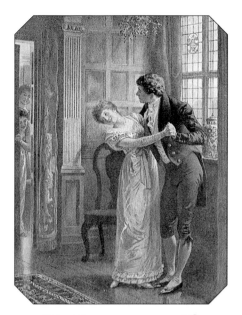

⇥❧ MISTLETOE ❧⇤

ITTING under the mistletoe
(Pale green, fairy mistletoe)
One last candle burning low,
All the sleepy dancers gone,
Just one candle burning on,
Shadows lurking everywhere :
Someone came, and kissed me there.

Tired I was; my head would go
Nodding under the mistletoe
(Pale green, fairy mistletoe)
No footstep came, no voice, but only,
Just as I sat there, sleepy, lonely,
Stooped in the still and shadowy air,
Lips unseen – and kissed me there.

WALTER DE LA MARE, 1873–1956

✦. A JIGGING PARTY ✦

THE guests had all assembled, and the tranter's party had reached that degree of development which accords with ten o'clock P.M. in rural assemblies. At that hour the sound of a fiddle in process of tuning was heard from the inner pantry.

"That's Dick," said the tranter. "That lad's crazy for a jig."

"Dick! Now I cannot—really, I cannot allow any dancing at all till Christmas day is out," said old William emphatically. "When the clock ha' done striking twelve, dance as much as ye like."

"Well, I must say there's reason in that, William," said Mrs. Penny. "If you do have a party on Christmas-day-night, 'tis only fair and honourable to the Church of England to have it a sit-still party. Jigging parties be all very well, and this, that, and therefore; but a jigging party looks suspicious. O, yes; stop till the clock strikes, young folk—so say I."

It happened that some warm mead accidentally got into Mr. Spinks's head about this time.

"Dancing," he said, "is a most strengthening, enlivening, and courting movement, especially with a little beverage added! And dancing is good. But why disturb what is ordained, Richard and Reuben, and the company zhinerally? Why, I ask, as far as that goes?"

"Then nothing till after twelve," said William.

Though Reuben and his wife ruled on social points, religious questions were mostly disposed of by the old man, whose firmness on this head quite counter-balanced a certain weakness in his handling of domestic matters. The hopes of the younger members of the household were therefore relegated to a distance of one hour and three-quarters—a result that took visible shape in them by a remote and listless look about the eyes—the singing of songs being permitted in the interim.

At five minutes to twelve the soft tuning was again heard in the back quarters; and when at length the clock had whizzed forth the last stroke, Dick appeared ready primed, and the instruments were boldly handled; old William very readily taking the bass-viol from its accustomed nail, and touching the strings as irreligiously as could be desired.

FROM *UNDER THE GREENWOOD TREE*
BY THOMAS HARDY, 1840–1928

O LITTLE TOWN OF BETHLEHEM

O LITTLE town of Bethlehem,
How still we see thee lie!
Above thy deep and dreamless sleep
The silent stars go by:
Yet in thy dark street shineth
The everlasting Light;
The hopes and fears of all the years
Are met in thee to-night.

O morning stars, together
Proclaim the holy birth,
And praises sing to God the King,
And peace to men on earth;
For Christ is born of Mary;
And, gathered all above,
While mortals sleep, the angels keep
Their watch of wondering love.

PHILLIPS BROOKS, 1835–1893

⊶ JOURNEY OF THE MAGI ⊷

"A COLD coming we had of it,
     Just the worst time of the year
For a journey, and such a long journey:
The ways deep and the weather sharp,
The very dead of winter."
And the camels galled, sore-footed, refractory,
Lying down in the melting snow.
There were times we regretted
The summer palaces on slopes, the terraces,
And the silken girls bringing sherbet.

Then the camel men cursing and grumbling
And running away, and wanting their liquor and women,
And the night-fires going out, and the lack of shelters,
And the cities hostile and the towns unfriendly
And the villages dirty and charging high prices:
A hard time we had of it.
At the end we preferred to travel all night,
Sleeping in snatches,
With the voices singing in our ears, saying
That this was all folly.

Then at dawn we came down to a temperate valley,
Wet, below the snow line, smelling of vegetation,
With a running stream and a water-mill beating the darkness,
And three trees on the low sky.
And an old white horse galloped away in the meadow.
Then we came to a tavern with vine-leaves over the lintel,
Six hands at an open door dicing for pieces of silver,
And feet kicking the empty wine-skins.
But there was no information, and so we continued
And arrived at evening, not a moment too soon
Finding the place; it was (you may say) satisfactory.

All this was a long time ago, I remember,
And I would do it again, but set down
This set down
This: were we led all that way for
Birth or Death? There was a Birth, certainly,
We had evidence and no doubt. I had seen birth and death,
But had thought they were different; this Birth was
Hard and bitter agony for us, like Death, our death.
We returned to our places, these Kingdoms,
But no longer at ease here, in the old dispensation,
With an alien people clutching their gods.
I should be glad of another death.

T. S. ELIOT, 1888–1965

⚜ THE GREAT WINTER ⚜

IT MUST have snowed most wonderfully to have made that depth of covering in about eight hours. For one of Master Stickles' men, who had been out all the night, said that no snow began to fall until nearly midnight. And here it was, blocking up the doors, stopping the ways, and the water courses, and making it very much worse to walk than in a saw-pit newly used. However, we trudged along in a line: I first, and the other men after me; trying to keep my track, but finding legs and strength not up to it. Most of all, John Fry was groaning; certain that his time was come, and sending messages to his wife, and blessings to his children. For all this time it was snowing harder than it ever had snowed before, so far as a man might guess at it; and the leaden depth of the sky came down, like a mine turned upside down on us. Not that the flakes were so very large; for I have seen much larger flakes in a shower of March, while sowing peas; but that there was no room between them, neither any relaxing, nor any change of direction.

Watch, like a good and faithful dog, followed us very cheerfully, leaping out of the depth, which took him over his back and ears already, even in the level places; while in the drifts he might have sunk to any distance out of sight, and never found his way up again. However, we helped him now and then, especially through the gaps and gateways; and so after a deal of floundering, some laughter, and a little swearing, we came all safe to the lower meadow, where most of our flock was hurdled.

But behold, there was no flock at all! None, I mean, to be seen anywhere; only at one corner of the field, by the eastern end, where the snow drove in, a great white billow, as high as a barn, and as broad as a house. This great drift was rolling and curling beneath the violent blast, tufting and combing with rustling swirls, and carved (as in

patterns of cornice) where the grooving chisel of the wind swept round. Ever and again the tempest snatched little whiffs from the channelled edges, twirled them round and made them dance over the chime of the monster pile, then let them lie like herring-bones, or the seams of sand where the tide has been. And all the while from the smothering sky, more and more fiercely at every blast, came the pelting, pitiless arrows, winged with murky white, and pointed with the barbs of frost.

But although for people who had no sheep, the sight was a very fine one (so far at least as the weather permitted any sight at all); yet for us, with our flock beneath it, this great mount had but little charm. Watch began to scratch at once, and to howl along the sides of it; he knew that his charge was buried there, and his business taken from him. But we four men set to in earnest, digging with all our might and main, shovelling away at the great white pile, and fetching it into the meadow. Each man made for himself a cave, scooping at the soft, cold flux, which slid upon him at every stroke, and throwing it out behind him, in piles of castled fancy. At last we drove our tunnels in (for we worked indeed for the lives of us), and all converging towards the middle, held our tools and listened.

FROM *LORNA DOONE* BY R. D. BLACKMORE, 1825–1900

✧ IN THE BLEAK MID-WINTER ✧

In the bleak mid-winter,
  Frosty wind made moan,
Earth stood hard as iron,
  Water like a stone;
Snow had fallen, snow on snow,
  Snow on snow,
In the bleak mid-winter,
  Long ago.

Our God, heaven cannot hold Him,
  Nor earth sustain;
Heaven and earth shall flee away
  When He comes to reign:
In the bleak mid-winter
  A stable-place sufficed
The Lord God Almighty,
  Jesus Christ.

CHRISTINA GEORGINA ROSSETTI, 1830–1894

🔊. TO CLIVE BELL 🔊

Lelant Hotel, Lelant,
[Cornwall]
26th Dec [1909]

MY DEAR CLIVE

It is past nine o'clock, and the people still sing carols beneath my window, which is open, owing to the clemency of the night. I am at the crossroads, and at the centre of the gossip of the village. The young men spend most of the day leaning against the wall, and sometimes spitting. Innumerable hymns and carols issue from barns and doorsteps. Several windows, behind which matrons sit, are red and yellow, and a number of couples are wandering up and down the roads, which shine dimly. Then there is the [Godrevy] lighthouse, seen as through steamy glass, and a grey flat where the sea is. There is no moon, or stars, but the air is soft as down, and one can see trees on the ridge of the road, and the shapes of everything without any detail. No one seems to have any wish to go to bed. They circle aimlessly. Is this going on in all the villages of England now? After dinner is a very pleasant time. One feels in the mood for phrases, as one sits by the fire, thinking how one staggered up Tren Crom in the mist this afternoon, and sat on a granite tomb on the top, and surveyed the land, with the rain dripping against one's skin. There are—as you may remember—rocks comparable to couchant camels, and granite gate posts, with a smooth turf road between them. Thinking it over is the pleasant thing....

FROM *THE FLIGHT OF THE MIND, THE LETTERS OF VIRGINIA WOOLF, 1888–1912*

⤙❦ REELING ON ICE ❦⤚

LD Wardle led the way to a pretty large sheet of ice; and the fat boy and Mr. Weller, having shovelled and swept away the snow which had fallen on it during the night, Mr. Bob Sawyer adjusted his skates with a dexterity which to Mr. Winkle was perfectly marvellous and described circles with his left leg, and cut figures of eight, and inscribed upon the ice, without once stopping for breath, a great many other pleasant and astonishing devices, to the excessive satisfaction of Mr. Pickwick, Mr. Tupman, and the ladies: which reached a pitch of positive enthusiasm, when old Wardle and Benjamin Allen, assisted by the aforesaid Bob Sawyer, performed some mystic evolutions, which they called a reel.

All this time, Mr. Winkle, with his face and hands blue with the cold, had been forcing a gimlet into the soles of his feet, and putting his skates on, with the points behind, and getting the straps into a very complicated and entangled state, with the assistance of Mr. Snodgrass, who knew rather less about skates than a Hindoo. At length, however, with the assistance of Mr. Weller the unfortunate skates were firmly screwed and buckled on, and Mr. Winkle was raised to his feet.

"Now, then, sir," said Sam, in an encouraging tone; "off with you, and show 'em how to do it."

"Stop, Sam, stop!" said Mr. Winkle, trembling violently, and clutching hold of Sam's arms with the grasp of a drowning man. "How slippery it is, Sam."

"Not an uncommon thing upon ice, sir," replied Mr. Weller. "Hold up, sir!"

This last observation of Mr. Weller's bore reference to a demonstration Mr. Winkle made at the instant, of a frantic desire to throw his feet in the air, and dash the back of his head on the ice.

"These–these–are very awkward skates; ain't they, Sam?" inquired Mr. Winkle, staggering.

"I'm afeerd there's a orkard gen'l'm'n in 'em, sir," replied Sam.

"Now, Winkle," cried Mr. Pickwick, quite unconscious that there was anything the matter. "Come; the ladies are all anxiety."

"Yes, yes," replied Mr. Winkle, with a ghastly smile. "I'm coming."

FROM *THE PICKWICK CLUB*
BY CHARLES DICKENS, 1812–1870

ᏍᎦ RING OUT WILD BELLS ᏍᎦ

RING out wild bells to the wild sky,
　　The flying cloud, the frosty light:
　　The year is dying in the night;
Ring out, wild bells, and let him die.

Ring out the old, ring in the new,
　　Ring, happy bells, across the snow:
　　The year is going, let him go;
Ring out the false, ring in the true.

Ring out old shapes of foul disease,
　　Ring out the narrowing lust of gold;
　　Ring out the thousand wars of old,
Ring in the thousand years of peace.

Ring in the valiant man and free,
　　The larger heart, the kindlier hand;
　　Ring out the darkness of the land,
Ring in the Christ that is to be.

FROM *IN MEMORIAM*
BY ALFRED, LORD TENNYSON, 1809–1892

⊰❄ HOME FOR CHRISTMAS ❄⊱

THIS is meeting time again. Home is the magnet. The winter land roars and hums with the eager speed of return journeys. The dark is noisy and bright with late-night arrivals–doors thrown open, running shadows on snow, open arms, kisses, voices and laughter, laughter at everything and nothing. Inarticulate, giddying and confused are those original minutes of being back again. The very familiarity of everything acts like shock. Contentment has to be drawn in slowly, steadyingly, in deep breaths–there is so much of it. We rely on home not to change, and it does not, wherefore we give thanks. Again Christmas: abiding point of return. Set apart by its mystery, mood and magic, the season seems in a way to stand outside time. All that is dear, that is lasting, renews its hold on us: we are home again. . . .

FROM *HOME FOR CHRISTMAS* BY ELIZABETH BOWEN, 1899-1973

ᘒᕲ ACKNOWLEDGEMENTS ᘓᕲ

TEXT ACKNOWLEDGEMENTS

The Publishers are grateful to all of the following for permission to reprint their copyright material in Penhaligon's *Christmas*.

Page 16 Extract from *Cider with Rosie* by Laurie Lee reprinted by permission of the author and The Hogarth Press, London ; 28 Extract from *King Cotton* by Thomas Armstrong, Collins Publishers, London ; 30 ' Christmas' © John Betjeman, reprinted by permission of Curtis Brown Ltd ; 34 Extract from *A London Child of the 1870s* by M. V. Hughes, 1934, Oxford University Press ; 52 Extract from ' A Prospect of the Sea' in *The Collected Stories of Dylan Thomas*, reprinted by permission of J. M. Dent & Sons Ltd, London, US copyright © by New Directions Publishing Corporation, reprinted by permission of New Directions, New York ; 79 Extract from *Shaw's Music* reprinted by permission of The Society of Authors on behalf of the Bernard Shaw Estate ; 80 Extract from ' The Dead' in *The Dubliners* by James Joyce reprinted by permission of the publishers Jonathon Cape Ltd, London and The Society of Authors as the literary representative of the Estate of James Joyce, US copyright 1916 by B.W. Huebsch, Inc., Definitive text copyright © 1967 by the estate of James Joyce, all rights reserved, reprinted by permission of Viking Penguin, a division of Penguin Books USA, Inc ; 82 Extract from *Little Grey Rabbit's Christmas* by Alison Uttley, illustrated by Margaret Tempest, 1940, Collins Publishers, London ; 83 ' Mistletoe' reprinted by permission of The Literary Trustees of Walter de la Mare and The Society of Authors as their representative ; 90 ' Journey of the Magi' reprinted by permission of Faber and Faber Ltd from *Collected Poems 1909-1962* by T. S. Eliot, US copyright 1936 Harcourt Brace Jovanovich Inc. and copyright © 1963, 1964 by T. S. Eliot, reprinted by permission of the publishers ; 99 Extract from *The Flight of the Mind, The Letters of Virginia Woolf, Vol 1, 1888-1912*, edited by Nigel Nicolson and Joanne Trautman, copyright © 1975 Quentin Bell and Angelica Garnett and reprinted by permission of Harcourt Brace Jovanovich Inc., New York, The Hogarth Press, London, and The Executors of the Virginia Woolf Estate ; 106 Extract from *Home For Christmas* by Elizabeth Bowen © 1957 by Prentice-Hall Inc., reprinted by permission of the author and Curtis Brown Ltd.

PICTURE ACKNOWLEDGEMENTS

Bridgeman Art Library:
Page 1 Father Christmas with Reindeer and Sleigh : Anon/Private Collection ;
5 Victorian Christmas card : Anon ; 8 A Fine Vintage : Gerard Portielje/Private Collection ; 9 Winter Scene : Anon ; 10-11 Home Sweet Home : Walter Dendy Sadler/Private Collection ; 14 Christmas card : Anon/Private Collection ; 33 The Poultry Seller : Petrus van Schendel/By Courtesy of Christie's, London ; 39 The Reverend Robert Walker Skating : Sir Henry Raeburn/National Gallery of Scotland, Edinburgh ; 40 The Mystic Nativity (detail of inside the stable) : Sandro Botticelli/ National Gallery, London ; 41 Contentment : Adolf Eberle/Josef Mensing Gallery. Hamm-Rhynern, West Germany ; 44 The Dish of Oysters : Jacob Ochtervelt/Harold Samuel Collection, Corporation of London ; 46-7 Napoleon III and The Empress Eugenie with the Court of the Second Empire Skating in the Bois de Bologne/ Collection of Christopher Forbes ; 51 The Nativity : Gerrit Van Honthorst/Galleria Degli, Uffizi, Florence ; 54 Christmas Sweets : Anon/Private Collection ; 55 The Artist's Two Youngest Sisters : Carl-Christian ; Constantin Hansen/Nordiska Museet ; 57 Father Christmas with Children : Karl Rogers/Victoria and Albert Museum ; 61 Christmas Turkey : Sophie Anderson/Private Collection ; 63 The

Christmas Hamper : Robert Braithwaite Martineau/Private Collection ; 65 A Winter
Skating Scene : Adriaen Pietersz van de Venne/Johnny van Haeften Gallery,
London ; 69, 71 The Christmas Tree : Albert Chevalier Tayler/Alexander Gallery,
London ; 73 Happy Christmas : Viggo Johansen/Hirsch Sprungske Collection,
Copenhagen ; 76 Christmas Morning at the Mast Head : William Small/Private
Collection ; 78 Cheers for the Navy : Anon/Private Collection ; 81 The Corner of the
Table : Paul Chabas/Musee Des Beaux Arts, Tourcoing/Giraudon ; 89 Our Lady
Worshipping the Child : Antonio Correggio/Galleria Degli, Uffizi, Florence ;
90 Journey of the Magi : Benozzo Gozzoli/Palazzo Medici-Riccardi, Florence ;
92-3 Adoration of the Magi : Andrea Mantegna/Private Collection ; 95 The Sun had
closed the Winter's Day : Joseph Farquharson/Towneley Hall Art Gallery and
Museum, Burnley ; 97 The Holly Cart : William Stone/Fine Art Investments,
London ; 98 A Winter's Evening : Caroline F. Williams/Oscar and Peter Johnson Ltd.,
London ; 105 a Frozen River Landscape : Jan Van de Capelle/Private Collection ; 107
Convalescent : Jules Emile Saintin.

Fine Art Photographic Library:
Page 2 Father Christmas filling stockings : Anon ; 3 Christmas : George Sheridan
Knowles ; 7 Christmas Dreams by the Fireside : Anon ; 13 Sounds of Revelry :
Augustus E. Mulready ; 15 Resisting Temptation outside The Punch Bowl :
J.H. Parkyn ; 16 School children playing in the snow : Jan Mari Ten Kate ; 17 Carol
Singing : Anon ; 18-19 Glad Tidings : William M. Spittle ; 22-3 Detected : John Callcott
Horsley R.A. ; 24 The Giant Snowball : Jean Mayne ; 25 The First Snow : Hermann
Sondermann ; 26-7 A Meeting in the Snow : Frederick Marianus Kruseman ; 28
Joyeux Noel : Anon ; 29 The Toy Shop : Thomas Benjamin Kennington ; 30 A Busy
Evening, Westminster Bridge and Parliament : Anon ; 34 A London Street, Winter
1907 : W. Ashwood ; 35 Ludgate Hill and St. Paul's Cathedral : Anon ; 36-7
Copenhagen, Ostergade at Christmas Time, 1890 : Erik Henningsen ; 48 Santa Claus
Arrives : Anon ; 49 Father Christmas : Anon ; 53 Christmas, The Artist's Son in the
studio : Otto Haslund ; 56 Christmas Eve : Walter Anderson ; 66-7 The Wassail Bowl :
Walter Dendy Sadler ; 68 Best Wishes for A Merry Christmas : Anon ; 83 Under the
Mistletoe : Edward Frederick Brewtnall ; 84 The Oyster Eaters : Attributed to Johann
Peter Hasenclever ; 85 Dancing to the Fiddle : Eugenio Zampighi ; 88 The Ferry :
Charles Theodore Frere ; 96 Shepherding in a Snow Storm : Mabel F. Messer ; 100
Winter Fun : Frank Dadd ; 101 Snowball Fight : Anon ; 102-3 Skating in St. James's
Park : John Ritchie ; 104 Hark The Herald Angels Sing : Anon ; 106 Arriving at the
Inn : Anon.

Delaware Art Museum: 79 Hesterna Rosa : Dante Gabriel Rossetti/Samuel & Mary R.
Bancroft Memorial.

Collins Publishers: 82 'The Kissing Bunch' illustration by Margaret Tempest

e.t. archive: 6 Christmas card c.1890 : Rosina Emmett/Victoria and Albert Museum

Illustrated London News Picture Library: 110-11.

Mary Evans Picture Library: 20 A Christmas Tree Fairy : Lizzie Mack ; 60 Stirring
the Christmas Pudding : Anon ; 72 Christmas cake : Thomas Crane ; 74 Children
Pulling a Cracker : Anon, 75 Blind Man's Buff : St. Clair Simmonds.

Sonia Halliday and Laura Lushington: 50 The St. Catherine Window, Christ Church
Oxford : Edward Burne-Jones.

The Marquess of Bath, Longleat House: 58-9 William Brooke, 10th Earl of Cobham
and his family : Hans Eworth.

The National Gallery, London: 43 The Virgin of the Rocks (detail) : Leonardo da
Vinci

The Tate Gallery: 86-7 Alleluia : Thomas Gotch.

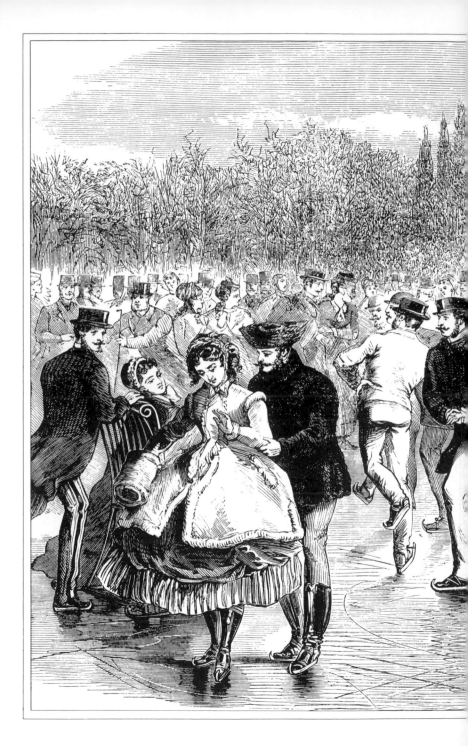

PENHALIGON'S
AT HOME
THE WINTER GARDEN

PENHALIGON'S Book of Christmas is scented with The Winter Garden which we introduced for Christmas last year. We developed it especially for use in the Autumn and Winter when the garden is no longer producing fragrant blossoms for use indoors. With its spicy notes of cloves and cinnamon and small fir cones, it is reminiscent of hot toddies and log fires and guaranteed to add a festive air.

Published in the United States by Harmony Books,
a division of Crown Publishers, Inc.,
225 Park Avenue South, New York, New York 10003

Published in Great Britain by Pavilion Books Limited

HARMONY and colophon are trademarks of
Crown Publishers, Inc.

Manufactured in Hong Kong

Library of Congress Catalog Card Number 89-1905

ISBN 0-517-57367-9

10 9 8 7 6 5

For more information about Penhaligon's
perfumes, please write to :
PENHALIGON'S
41 Wellington Street
Covent Garden
London WC2